3 130035 616

CW01072715

Please return/renew this item by the last date shown

OXFORDSHIRE
COUNTY COUNCIL
LEISURE & ARTS

THE UNDERTOW

The UNDERTOW
NEW AND SELECTED POEMS

JOHN KINSELLA

PUBLICATIONS
1996

Published by Arc Publications
Nanholme Mill, Shaw Wood Road
Todmorden, Lancs., OL14 6DA

Text copyright © John Kinsella 1996
Introduction copyright © Michael Hulse 1996
Copyright © Arc Publications 1996

Design by Tony Ward
Printed at Arc & Throstle Press
Nanholme Mill, Todmorden, Lancs.

ISBN 1 900072 07 8

Acknowledgments:
The publishers wish to thank Fremantle Arts
Centre Press, Australia for permission to
reprint poems.

The author wishes to acknowledge that some
of these poems were written while he was a
recipient of Fellowships from the Literature
Board of the Australia Council, and Creative
Development grants from the W.A.
Department for the Arts. He also wishes to
acknowledge the following journals for poems
included in the fourth section of this volume:
Hobo, Meanjin, Nimrod (USA), *Scripsi,
Southerly, The Iowa Review* (USA), *The West
Australian, Ulitarra,* and *Verse.*

The publishers acknowledge assistance from
Yorkshire and Humberside Arts Board.

Arc Publications International Poets:
Series Editor: Michael Hulse

JOHN KINSELLA was born in 1963 in Perth, Western Australia. After studying at the University of Western Australia, he travelled extensively through Europe and Asia. He has lived and worked in rural Western Australia, been the recipient of grants and fellowships from the W.A. Department for the Arts and the Literature Board of the Australia Council, and published in journals throughout the world. He was recently awarded one of the inaugural Young Australian Creative Fellowships for "outstanding artistic contribution to the nation". He is the founding editor of the poetry journal *Salt* and the small press *Folio*.

Contents

FOREWORD

John Kinsella, born in the same year as Simon Armitage, is the rising star of Australian poetry. Mercurial, gifted, wired, he has collected awards as a desk drawer collects paper clips. He has attracted the attention of readers as unlike as Harold Bloom, Lyn Hejinian and Les Murray. John Tranter and Philip Mead, selecting for their recent *Bloodaxe Book of Modern Australian Poetry*, chose him as their younger statesman, the anchor man of an anthology that emphasized the postmodern in Oz.

Critics have been quick to note that two bodies of work exist side by side in Kinsella's writing. Lyn Hejinian, distinguishing between the "meditative, narrative" and the "experimental", goes on to suggest that the difference is in fact an epistemological or temporal one. It is a point well made. Even so, I think Les Murray's famous distinction between the Athenian and the Boeotian is more fruitful in understanding Kinsella.

The Athenian is the urban-minded culture of sophistication, of modern and metropolitan values as opposed to the traditional-minded, ruder, more provincial and rural Boeotian values. In John Kinsella this division is apparent in parallel sets of loyalties: to the world of innovative art and poetry (Muybridge, Warhol, Duncan, Prynne) but also to the claims of tradition (Shakespeare, Cowley, and I suspect, the Virgil of the *Eclogues*); to the metropolitan climate of analytic discourse (Kinsella's poems are clearly *au courant* with contemporary theory) but also to the importance of being versed in country things. With his parrots and plums, his farm talk and his understanding of farmers' ways in Western Australia, Kinsella is certainly "an anamnesis of rural Australia," and indeed "unafraid to honour it with the full stretch of his language," as Les Murray has said; but in poems such as the *Syzygy* sequence or the more recent 'Erratum', though rural vocabulary remains, the poet's mind clearly moves to another music.

This selection gives readers in Britain a first opportunity to make the fuller acquaintance of this arresting writer. The pleasures he offers vary enormously: beside the essentially contemplative, accessible and almost pastoral poems which appear in the first and third sections here, there are others that will not grant easy access. I have yet to meet a reader who can formulate a coherent account of what is going on in *Syzygy*; but equally, I have yet to meet a reader who failed to be excited by the electric crackle that runs through that sequence, and the sheer bravado of the writing. There are poems in this selection in which Kinsella keeps company with Frost; there are others in which he might as well be Charles Olson on a bad trip. One thing is certain: he is not making things too easy for us. And we must read him entire.

A word about the text. The poems in the first section are selected from *Eschatologies* (Fremantle Arts Centre Press, 1991) and *Full Fathom Five* (Fremantle Arts Centre Press, 1993). The second section gives the text of *Syzygy* (Fremantle Arts Centre Press, 1993) entire. The third is chosen from *The Silo* (Fremantle Arts Centre Press, 1995). In the fourth, three poems – 'Self-Portrait without Glasses', 'A (C)ode for Simon Templar' and 'Erratum' – are from his latest Australian collection, *Erratum/ Frame(d)* (Folio/Fremantle Arts Centre Press, 1995), while the remaining poems in that section are previously uncollected. A very few self-evident misprints in the original texts have been silently corrected; but words or coinages that exist only in the pages of John Kinsella have of course been left.

Michael Hulse
March 1996

I

INLAND: early poems

Full Fathom Five

On viewing a reproduction of *Full Fathom Five* in Ellen G. Landau's *Jackson Pollock*, and thinking over the recent death of a friend by drowning.

Full fathom five thy father lies;
     Of his bones are coral made;
Those are pearls that were his eyes.
     Nothing of him that doth fade
But doth suffer a sea change
     Into something rich and strange.
          The Tempest, Act 1, scene ii. Shakespeare.

Five fathoms out there. Full fathom five thy father lies. At once he said. Found drowned. High water at Dublin bar. Driving before it a loose drift of rubble, fanshoals of fishes, silly shells. A corpse rising saltwhite from the undertow, bobbing landward, a pace a pace a porpoise. There he is. Hook it quick. Sunk though he be beneath the watery floor. We have him. Easy now.
          Ulysses, James Joyce.

1

Gallery-wise it rates
as a painting
of unfathomable depth.
On my desk it is the surface
of both a puddle or an ocean.
As they say, you can drown
in both.

2

I've a great uncle who captained
a bullion ship
which capsized during a storm
rounding the Horn. These
the 'eroded treasures'
noted by Landau
as occurring in the swells
and rips of paint?

3

There he is. Hook it quick.

Full fathom five
dredged deep
the glory
of drowning
in a river
or taking to sea
and being dragged
back to shore.
The hook as sharp
as sight honed
by shamans,
the corpse a prismatic
reflection
of the living body.

Chaotic fish
dissect currents,
dislocate reefs,
and scatter sandbanks.
They will not be recruited
as pallbearers.

4

Full? What if the ocean's floor
is fluxive? A mixture
of excrement and bone,
lime-slurry and sand,
mud and decaying tissue?
Full fathom five
multiplied. The formula
variable. A multi-storied
apartment or funeral

parlour? If so
the basement
is never featured
in the catalogues
or brochures.

5

Full fathom five
the eyes burn
the undertow,
state-changing: vaporous,
liquid, solid.
A body's flow-down
arrests pollution, death
a notion of the surface.
I submerge the image.

6

Pebbles and tacks
pennies and buttons
a pair of keys
combs and matches
cigarettes and paint
tube tops
fallen overboard
and swallowed
by dense sweeps
of effluent
and colouring
agents.

7.

In finding his way
Pollock may have joined
the path of suicides,
the ocean a forest
through which you
approach the circles
of Inferno (molten,
drenched in spirits).
The jewels of distortion
shine in the blue-green
flurries, and the wreckage
of a brief life unwinds
the silver threads
of darkness.

Eclogue on a Well

She stirs the waters
breaking the stone rust surface;
if the branch she holds
were longer she might
bring proof to the claim
that more than one surface
lies beneath. Even so, I defer
to her belief that the One
is solid ground – the reflection
of a deep well in a dry field.

Pipeline

The pipeline cleaves the catchment
with its good intention – on a watersling
outflowing the silver jacket, palmed
off by pumping station after pumping
station, though losing none of its spring,
darting forwards with a hop, skip, and a jump,
riding sidecar to a national highway,
swinging from one climate to another
without a change of expression.
                              An egret flies
lower over a coastal reservoir, parrots
in unclaimed territory know the pipeline
to be a hot cable that will burn through claw,
a crow senses moisture at the final
pumping station.
                    In passing, it remains
indifferent to farm machinery, to the crisp
and wink of saltpans, to finches tossing
their hoods back and tittering
about its stiff shell.
                    In passing, it gloats inwardly
before leaving a dry wind that's been shooting
its skin to wrestle with scrub, before plunging
headfirst into red earth.

At the Serpentine Pipehead

Defrocked camellias,
their discarded skirts
rotting in unceremonious heaps –
The Water Board hopes you have
enjoyed your visit, welcomes
suggestions – I suggest the plum flower,
the almond blossom . . . I suggest the song
of a lorikeet cast like a net
through the deadwood of spent trees,
I suggest the area closed off
because of dangerous chemicals,
I suggest the solitary catboat,
its limp sail a premonition,
a marooned pilotless ferry
on the distant bank.

Crossing the wall of the small pipehead
a child crouches to view the waters,
through the space between fence
and concrete – the green mesh confusing
the picture, preventing pure vision.
I trace the lime-sweat tributaries:
spread like bruised capillaries
they broach the hairline cracks of the walkway.
I admire the lichen welding the walls:
no talus-creep, these rocks have fallen neatly
into place, though the position of hills
and filtered river is by chance.

Inland

Inland: storm tides,
ghosts of a sheep weather
alert, the roads uncertain

families cutting the outback
gravel on Sunday mornings,
the old man plying the same track
to and from the session
those afternoons, evenings
(McHenry skidded into a thickset
mallee after a few too many
and was forced to sell up)

On the cusp of summer
an uncertain breeze
rises in grey wisps
over the stubble –
the days are ashen,
moods susceptible,
though it does not take
long to get back
into the swing of things

We take the only highroad
for miles as the centre
of the primum mobile – it's
the eye of the needle
through which our lives'
itineraries must be drawn,
a kind of stone theodolite
measuring our depths beyond
the straight and narrow,
it's a place of borrowed dreams
where the marks of the spirit
have been erased by dust –
the restless topsoil

Plumburst
for Wendy

The neat greens of Monument Hill
roll into sea, over the rise the soft rain
of plumfall deceives us in its groundburst.

If lightning strikes from the ground up,
and Heaven is but an irritation that prompts
its angry spark, then plums are born
dishevelled on the ground and rise
towards perfection . . .

Out of the range of rising plums
we mark the territory of the garden,
testing caprock with Judas trees,
pacing out melon runs. Behind us a block
of flats hums into dusk and the sun
bursts a plum mid-flight.

Foxes and Python

A fox skin
in a nitrate bath,
and a fox skin drying
stiff as a card
folded over the levers
of a veteran plough,
stare fixedly at a python
coiled about the lintel
of the sheep shed – 'comes
down about once a month
for a feed', the farmer says,
pleased that it remains,
having appeared, like the foxes,
'out of the blue one day'.

Carcass of Sheep in Fork of Dead Tree

A set up. The carcass slung
over a fork in a dead tree,
the line-of-sight unbroken
from shearing shed, perfect
for high powered rifles
with telescopic lenses
hungry for *predators*. You see,
certain birds think nothing
of rotting sheep climbing
dead trees. Nor, at a later
date, when the ribcage
has become the staves
of an ark stranded by flood,
of a photographer convincing
his subject to sit naked
beneath the wreckage, the grey
branches – side stretched
such that the nipple closest
to the camera becomes
as sharp as the eye
    a bullet.

Strange Metaphors

'Isn't he the guy who uses strange metaphors – like
describing cars with teeth?'

Anthony Lawrence

Collapse is wild with symmetry
and mechanical savants move with artistic
hands – making poetry out of the angry
expressions of car grills. The drinks
waiter steps in just in the nick of time
and offers a vision of a sturgeon sailing
through flaccid waters driven by an ambient
wind, getting no further than the length
of its entrails. The clean-shaven makes
a cameo appearance, the grey barrel suit
setting the forget-me-not off perfectly.
After all, we are poets, and have got to be
able to make sense of this. Look! Quickly
the wedge-tailed eagle takes leave of its
broken body – no time to waste, it's a long flight
back to the Nullarbor. And, great joy, the day
is ours – watch Ashbery dip into a hint of Rilke
and lodge himself delicately amongst our words.
Though let's be wary and not display the trophy
yet – somebody at a distant table is suggesting
that there's more than a hint of ghost writer
about this, that strange metaphors have been
forced to do their captor's bidding.

Sexual Politics in Eadweard Muybridge's
Man Walking, after Traumatism of the Head

1

He could easily be
A man walking, after traumatism
Of the head.
There's something vaguely Platonic about this.
Francis Bacon, lip-synching
His way through smugness, injecting passion and/or lust
Into Muybridge's studies of wrestlers: 'Actually,
Michelangelo and Muybridge
Are mixed up in my
Mind together, and so I perhaps
Could learn about positions
From Muybridge
And learn about the ampleness,
The grandeur of form
From Michelangelo …' This is not tongue-in-cheek,
And why should it be she cries?
At the end of the day
Folly counts for nothing, she says
Majestically, the banana light glowing
Sedately by the bedhead, Foucault
Powerless and fading.

2

What moral autonomy remains
As, from frame to frame,
He walks. Why aren't you a panel beater?
She asks as your last thought spills
To the floor and scatters.

Muybridge considered
Leland Stanford's Quest To Prove
All Four Legs Of A Trotting Horse
Are Off The Ground Simultaneously
At A Particular Moment ... earlier
He'd been a fly on the wall
As Muybridge blew his wife's
Dashing, cavalier lover away ...
'omne animal triste post coitum'.

Sadness comes quickly
And he wonders about
The contents of his blood.
And panel beaters would find
The passive role
Difficult
To shape.

3

Sharing a cell with lust
In the prison of desire
He remarked that the form
Of his cell-mate was a little peculiar:
Casanova moving with the gait
Of one who has succumbed
To animal locomotion, an electro-photographic
Investigation of consecutive phases
Of animal movement.

She says that he measures progress
With his penis, a well-oiled dip stick:
Her body absorbing the entire jungle
Of his body which is ecologically sound,
Creeping out of its rich enclave
And seeking to make the barren lush.
He believes that you can't get off
On rape, that violence is mental
Sickness.
I like his manners – c'est tout –
She confesses.

4

A skull fractured
Does not necessarily
Mean liberation
On the afterdeath plane
Nor freedom for the oppressed mind.
LSD, a freak in drag,
Denies the mind is lodged
In the skull, that it is
Part of the body. The dozens or so
Blotters found in his pocket
Have nothing to do
With his portfolio
Of deviance.
He's on top of it,
And knows the yellow haze
Suppressing the landscape
Is merely ash
In the upper-atmosphere.
The signature is this: it hurts
To cum on bad acid, but did that
ever deter you?

5

His head is traumatised
By dehydration, his brain shrinking.
Starvation has frayed the linkages
Between spinal cortex and legs.
His walk is one of decline
Interrupted by hope.
He feels spent and thin.
Men eat to vomit and vomit to eat,
Seneca tells us, and no woman can be too rich or too thin.
Chastity is starvation
Starvation is traumatism of the head.

6

She hates the hype
But loves the splendour:
The page written she relinquishes
Her rights to the material
Inherently hers. The moral community
Is concerned only with growth
At the end of the day – he tells them
That he is hers and couldn't give a shit.
Does she reciprocate they say?
Would you – a man walking,
With a traumatism of the head?

7

Underwire bras and jockstraps
Entangle a chicken desperately
Lunging, a torpedo already
Within range of its tail feathers,
Rudely muzzling its way
Through a sea of discharge.
So, this is love? it asks.
Muybridge screams from his observation post
'Keep the bloody thing within the gridwork!
Calibrate, calibrate! for God's sake
It's all comparative.' Stripping off
He rushes the chicken and wrestles it,
'Damn the torpedoes, keep the cameras rolling!'
Duchamp's Nude descends a staircase
While Meissoner, de Neuville, Detaille,
Remington, Malevich, and Giacomo Balla,
Watch on excitedly.

8

When size doesn't matter
You'd better start asking questions.
I mean, it's all or nothing
Isn't it. As for what's behind it …
A magnet *does* have *two* poles.
Self control, the object of pleasure:
Every orgasm a spot in time
Without the lacework.

And this all about walking,
With a traumatism of the head,
The lexicon spread as three rednecks
Smash you over the skull with iron-knuckled
Fists, or an overdose of speed threatens
To burst capillaries, or glass lodged in a crescent
Below your left eye dislodges and unplugs
The contents of your identity.
The time lapse between frames shortens
And your collapse is traced
More minutely. Hasten slowly.

9

Porn is the Theory.
Rape is the Practice.
A sign held by a youth
In Minneapolis.
A skirt stained with sweat
Radiates in a bath
Of yellow dye.
The gate is locked,
The fences high.
She, sunbaking,
Looks over her shoulder,
Her tan slipping away:
In a tree perches
Her neighbour,
A glint in his eye.

10

Stripping thought,
He dreamt an anthology,
Visual and responsive.
Reflections on the obvious.
A spring day and I'm full of hate.
Stuff like that.
He would include
A photograph by Muybridge,
(Who after disposing of Major Larkyns
Apologised to the ladies
And settled to a newspaper).
Though not one of his locomotion
Sequences, whose implication
Goes beyond a book, but of the Colorado
In dry dock accompanied by an anonymous
Muybridge on Contemplation Rock
Later used as proof of madness.
And on the title page a quote
From The San Francisco Daily
Evening Post: 'Little
Did Muybridge dream
As he bent over
The bedside of his wife
And he caressed her,
That Larkyn's kisses
Were yet fresh and hot
Upon her lips'.

On Andy Warhol's *Marilyn Six-Pack*

Rip top lips – the movement is piracy.
An early cut – an addict's selective

disclosure. A perfect pose concealing
popular truths, the value of trashy

synthetic polymer makeup, canvas
skin and silkscreened hair. A six-pack's hazy

suppression of class and style, like seeing
the world in black and white. Quick! Look at me!

it pleads with a fizzing hiss. If you stand
long enough success will expose itself.

The pout shapes the plates, but the eyelids take
the weight – suspended languidly below

the constructed eyebrows. O Marilyn –
six tabs without the blister packaging.

II

Syzygy

1 Apprehension

And how did you feel
the surface too close
and the flappers fizzing
at your tender
and vulnerable
                    feet
loaded with misgivings?
Swift overload catapulting
recrimination
the largess culminating
cinema papers boys-own-annual-ing
from post office to mailbox
and bicycle-clip braces
on the maligned bull terrier's
teeth: an island of green
reticulated sucked into the soft pink
of the suburb, insurmountable the ratepayer's
anguish and bravado! the house a kraken
or bathysphere undercutting the plane,
adjunct to surface, one dimensional
suction. O fear ripples evading
sonar buoys Blue Gum Lake
receding as bores suck effluent
from beneath the arses of ducks.

Paperbarks turn black
water soils over
banks of sodden bread
and soft drink cans
this is popular viewing
medium small frame minutiae
chronic screen or inhabited pasture,
pointillist and contentious
cartooning serious ineptitudes
hatchback unravelling a bend
the lock-stock
barrelling it into sticky drink
at the bottom of the can: sure,
we feel strung up and depleted – light
even heavy and darkness uplifting,

37

necessitating remission into screaming
as the engine revs the flywheel
seems not to move dear o dear
love's texts spread haphazardly over the bucket
seats – and don't we know
they're braggarts! denying fusion
and invading asteroids, deploying
consumables and calling
it art.

2 Fallout

A refugee from contention I load
stills into the projector
taking the negative impression
adjuncting
expression prising anger
out of its folds
the damage budding retentive
small experiment releasing heat:
remember looting these impressions?
machinery expressive and light-
conscious love scarifying poise
the tractor rocketing the clods of loamy earth
bootlegging frustration mudbrick and fencewire
circular-saws threatening Robert Frosts
and doorpost jamming two years too old
and rotting, the sun orange plastic,
perfect, the film was black
and white and the sheep gurgling
hysterically.

3 Self-regard

-ing homonculous metals chambers
tinfoiling exclusions like humidicribs
wheeling slick asphalt deletions
and stripping film, dust water licking
axminster carpet spreadsheets – what shows
in the headlights or pinheaded

spotlight? Crunch. Synthetic victims.
And the frogs croak politely
in their ditches. HALT! Good year
wet weather halts the death of a zebra
just outside a butcher's shop. Can't read the signs
good who gives a damn anyway?
Needed, inquire within: good management
and sensible market indicators.
Those who leave anything up to description
need not remote opinions. Morality
stinks, we keep it in buckets.

4 When the flappers tickle your fancy

opposing needs, priming pellegra
with plastic cement like jelly rubber
singing aging movies, tall tales lugging drabness
out of forums: humitrophic, water glass
or sundial gas-bagging in the shade, Ah
such is fame passing the time. The car comes.
A stretch in tails. Silk doors predella
adjuncting talent AND the driver. Let us in!
Take us entire rhomboidal all and Oolala
susurrous through disconnexion, baffling
sibilance. O my flappers, what a team we make!
And the planets co-habitate and read life
impression, you have your strict
and your lax, the cups drink too much
and the television in the back of the limo
is stuck on the same channel. The driver
is sucking himself. Take no notice.
You are my family he splurges:
executors   guardians   trustees
receivers   inheritors
good sides half backs
flankers absorbers potentates
contrivers emissaries
agitators incarnations
lovers leaping onto the tired pile
of my flesh.

5 The Cane Cutter

Reflex take a breath.   ( )   A snake
operates amongst rough cane-cutter's crystalline sweat.
A particle overload.
Heavy rain bearing down
palpitating trifolate with sun and cane
no rainbow
makes an appearance.
Earthy very earthy. Miasma
camouflaged mud takes all takers
and throws back a marsh of fences.
They beg for tariffs. They like restrictions.
In the highlands water is lightning
gaping press-down and half bas-relief.
Turbine churn-out comes down
from highlife where the air is heady.
No fireflies there. Dowsed and riddled
deep deep south roots dry the bone-black
subterranean streams, raddled shapes forking azurine
on meeting archaeological light, spent swarming
the traps, for this is Ground Zero Warholing
in cyclone territory, zoning the sirens
equivocating hot dogs and pies mushrooms
pushed to the side of the plate: cadillacs
racketing Monroe hubcaps
currency cut like love
on a breezy day, hot air concentrating
in the sewers.

6 Life-driver

Placating pit swimmers
the bone mill splurgers
credit cards bursting middle-class prognosis
dialectic good will and science
is upon us bursting prognosis
good will tragacanth
imprint forms lotus form
the new behemoth, a signature naked
beneath the ultra-violet: rex regis

suppressing atoll watchers, spreading
blood and bone over the garden. Lair-down devil
lair down! Vrooom!

7 Subjecting objects to serious scrutiny

Draining absence as blue
trance stelazine melting circulars
                        restraining the abstract
                        fingerpainting
lithium to bind
Mono Mondrian on its platform of shape:
threatening construction on its very
printed page, corrector fluid
swashbuckling first words
formatted like a river ending
in a window mouse decorating
graphic disasters
without compassion. We impose.
Macrographic-Beta-Language.
And you don't even have to
drop names!
                    Advertising blimps
nudge traffic controllers pneumatic
in their agitating seats,
tattoos green with red tracers
running like hits. Here, disasters
falsetto screech *sus. per coll.*
like corporate suicide
across the polished screens.

8 The forest, the farm. a hybrid bathysphere

Lumped or polyglotted, mixing
but insistent on claustrophobic
limits, cans of repellent
stink like flypaper.
They undercut a fluid market
holding back the fragile forest,
rending tight-as-money-talk, marketeers

would cut sleepers where they stood:
Chinese whispers like nostalgia. Downburnt
the weird beast charts pressure, breath
contrivance as the water is fire:
volunteers roll back the pasture, the forest
corals and suffers. Greenhousing
the coldest waters, peepshow languishing
amongst saw-jawed lantern fish
surface molten, stripped of its cage.

9 Inflecting ambiguity / electric trains

A type of ambiguity
that carves the hissing wires
clouds volcanic on the scarp
as kids general motor it with a mania
that drives them East: surveillance
a seance partially materialising
voices from closets steel-faced
and never changing critics
like having a field day: tracks glisten
briefly like sin in its rage
cauterising
          rugged-up patrons waiting
for concert tickets outside
the entertainment centre
as staunch pylons share goods and flashes
with cameras and country trains, not electric
but still photogenic. Dispensation
of tickets as curricles dash past
and we celebrate the past.

10 Palpable Paludal – the defence rests

Palpable cacology – admit the document –
juggling heartburn
passing paludal intoxicants
adhesives and cleansing agents
out back the hardware store
supermarket strings strummed or struck

the plastic shopping bag dissolving
or blowing up like a lung,
thick and tumorous when breath whispers
triplicate super realist on super realist
zygal chevron zippered-up
the fire-escape rusted
and decompressed – the blossom
plucked while locked
in its cloak and cap, night-fruit
copping it sweet in daylight: our bodies
botanical: facades
as the tallest poppy
accepts the flak
its tinted window reflecting
it back, carbonaceous angels
triggering sumptuous sprinklers,
the housing estates sinking
into the swamp stomping
faddish death beats
only the well-heeled speak
borrowing cultural tid-bits
repackaged   tender   taste-sensitised
suppressing the threats.

11 Deletions

Fortitude rippling cross-sense-
a-round clip-board logic
accumulating detailing Harleys
like shepherds' calendars in the month
of January the heat was Cyrenaic and intense
displaced vermilion weathering
irregularities like windows
and quick assimilations, pique & niche,
lavender disaster soft and not in the slightest
mechanical – BUT deletion rakes
a monster making shape from less
than its constituents, well-made enigmas
propitiatory hermeneutic and well coded,
I differ camping on fault-lines highways upending
bridges siphoning rivers neuter

crushed velvet ripped from the dash,
die bobbing infra-red night sight slick like bedrock and pylons
congealed beneath town planners forgetting mud, acronym
comfortable city lazy body lay-about
the pool pretzels beer and much more: the 'staff of life'
single tracking compression and tidiness,
an accident absorbs clumping only
for publicity: obliquity luxuriant
first class dozer drivers machining silver spray
amyl nitrate staining fingers
in tills corporate gets-ya-goin' up and adam
furrowing nutrition and filling cavities.

12 Entropy / Flesh

Spontaneous bloodstock rattles and broods
lapping power-lifted pasture amidst
the fences – narcs and passive devourers of feed
immunising syringes. Meathood gestures gantries
and ramps while Soutine feeds love in a French
abattoir la la la B grade and trendy, rattle O three-tiered
calashes, looking brutal in the halogens, cauterising
debris up-ended white posts with red and silver
dazzlers lowering their lids, slipping on damp days
into the smell of wool and hide, mopping
placental blankets with rough tongues.
Window painting stretch addressing
ambulance and attendant starter motors
commensural commercial additives
like bolt guns stunning and electro-shock
on top of the hill beneath a liver-shaped moon
draining the blood from your nervous
system-ism, the spill-down lathering
the coronets of your contact-lenses, drainage inquiline
wearing it like a glove or
coating stomachs – STIFFEN UP LADS! the hoi
polloi tax-evading and avoiding road-blocks
born into banking liquids that solidify
with limb-movement, the floor
approaching rapidly: a Gnostic
logion: the fish nibbles my toes

and good it feels sovereign vessels toes & lips
divisive
hobnobbing
traipsing stainless on the whetstone   outcrop
sheep-weather-alert
or battery-bound and the wind chafing tinwalls
clocking the pulse of eggdrop and peelable wool
and udders performing ridiculous labours: supreme-O
a brand name marketable, affirmations corporate
conferring garnished parsley hints, staking
first grade glue sticks   how many shares?
brokered on the floor household cleansers
banish the addictive canvas, Ah tundra vista
the canvas captures and projects
the sky shocked and hooked
Mrs. McCarthy & Mrs. Brown
immobilised by Tuna fish, disaster spread
like emulsified stabilised sheen upon
Marilyn's tender lips c/- Big Sirs: Sir
of the pigskin briefcase, brylcream quinella
stated portfolio lapses pump-action
and blood-staked, entablature
en-loading your own quizzing sense-around. Smell it!
Singing western and roto broiling I've hooked a big one
bone black and threatening to move
quotes like numerous grains of dry powder
centrefire monumentalised 1080
vacuuming heat-sealed trophies skins
pre-packaged mise-en-scène urging texture
out of quadrature, arc the brittle black
cuttlefish, sepia toning cinemas
flensing storage facilities, you drag
something up out of memory and into sight.
Steaming black frost cleansing sun deliciously sharp
and breakfasting on the damp patio, lush tallow
candle canopying shades and predicting a good
hard-humping sunset. Progenate policedog
physiology derived and detecting goals
evaluating hereditary from 'weaning to slaughter'
heterozygous random carcass the beauty
collapses, Santayana might have been ugly.

45

13 Ripples

Streaming blue divisions, sections
of the neighbourhood, the lights of Canning Vale
ludicrous sporting brilliance rainslicks
like the MCG and gracing a stadium of cages –
Movietone ships sink and planes disperse
in black strategy, walk-on parts erotically
developing & reproducing cryptic typologies;
passion active and unassailable, declaring
intermittently, rippling like the skin
of persons or sulo-bins rattled by traffic,
city initiated carnivale for officers
on chilly Autumn nights eking out nostalgia
clumped together at the same scene long after
the bang, roadgame, cosmic microwave
background radiation as the fighter plane
sends tracers spitting into columns
of uniformly spread refugees: organisation
saves none of them.

14 Trigger

Yoke the vicious integer, sun and moon
uncomfortably syzygetic: 'Deep Throat'
shifting consensus, plead your case
and get the hell out of here. I won't
listen anyway! The quadrature sets limits
AND appeals X pronto. Things don't stick
unless they're forced to. No couples
can sit comfortably here: rekindling
love-on-a-pier, the car humming
on a verge or aiming for the country
downwind and forgetful upending the heart
off-loading blots of anger a clock chimes
in a mall of pastiche. Trigger, I fall
collecting apogean multiples of disorder.

15 Landfall / The Collapse of Beauty

Loose materials patterning sundials
at water's edge: embracing saline
trend/'/s crystalline fatigues
-loss- myriad system
-is-ation
interest vis à vis
disintegral compendiums, oil-slick
& refuse & foam casually concocting
beneath an historic swing bridge
a couple of hours [drive fro]m Perth, up-river
skiers hacking the lower
reaches
and paddocks might appear
mostly folds of beauty
– tourists understand this! – satisfying
rare inner-city creatures marooned
passive purposeful indulgently
headlines might claim.

16 Chemical

Boom-arm pod-fed nuzzles teaming foam
out over red earth: new machines
churning chemical seas in-lateral drift-a-round
phenomenally hand-in-hand with tractors
and deranged furrows rippling
heavy clods of soil
                    run-off creek river sea
deranged furrowing residual
        when myth hits purchase
who wants clean food?
bulimic south anorexic mid-point
        dr i p-fed north
deep-inhaling flyspray
and mosquito coils
fr - ie - ze dried coffee
cleaning a particularly
stubborn stove or bad guests
from a party.

47

17 First Blood

Tubed out of you warm and recycled cold.
Flow impedes logic cold as stain-
less steel like a disinterested object
of beauty, sun-bathing internal solarium
blood ultra'd & raddled
re: transfusion. Dizzy float extracts
inflatables, double toxicological
cell-sized machines making repairs
restructuring walls disengaged
by injective inter-ex-change
blood money breathes
franchise fantastic voyage
efficient redistribution
for this they test. byo.
branching profusely
gaining the respect
of ambulance drivers
slamming T-bar automatics gloved
and averting, petrol-guzzling
monsters finned and beautiful
gybing through your sanguine &
unguent utterings
staunch against venomous
        '{Dais de l'oeil revulse}'
bathe five death on red/s: (a) disaster
guilt feud bath (h)ound letting lust sport
thirsty money-stained sucker
auspicate consanguinity
rarely colourless or violently positive
genealogy suppurating
my grandfather fell
into the offal pit: Benny's Bonemill
        circa
1923.

18 peine forte et dure

What pleads 'I'
in the gloom, of
bulb-blow
& ocean-carpet
closing shore
lee & lea
to hills
a sprinkle of desquamating quartz
      sun-dank
spent
                  re-flex-ive
though who owns the fragments (?)

19 Gloat

who   lives by
    lies by
and
buy re-active blood/y
mis-fortune
assigned Con tra Dik shuns
an audience despite their buying
    him drinks
pneumatics taxonomy dialectics
    & quark of despair.

20 Feedback

Charles (O)lson
'Not one death but memor
   ot accumulation but change, the feedback is
the   aw

21 Fume

Soil tactless infuses
dust-cradles　*　objectifies
black frost on breathing land
fuming. anger military
pro fuse　Ion deficient
upper upper　flight
developing a dislike
for 'us': the bulldozers
have sweet tooths & fume.

22 Float – ing

(i)
Respond
float-ing soil
heresy
and the fog
absorbs pink-quartz
thrust-drift.

(ii)
Tractor churns heavy
despotic bones: sheep anatomy
undering edgy discs
and salty furrows luminous
night-work
driver's red-neck hurts.

(iii)
Fencing wire coils
snakes complex
in gullies

crops
and wild radishes
rot.

(iv)
Scour stalk-base and stubble
vast rimmed fields
charred in waves,
ash-water lapping
like gout: first rains
float.

23 Narrative

(i) telescope: passive

Up in the hills / closer: week (end) tours
not the building you'd think
[though] they've made
the right moves in the foyer. The
predicate fails to leave, we assume
via adjustin gth efoca llen g th
that he's always been (t)here! Zeiss
optics.

(ii) the night sky might be an all day sucker

take down [to] flatlands the jigger
of nostalgia – a few slides lo-priority
& secure. they call him Kid. hey Kid
cop a load of the moon} loud in his
ear pricking with chilly air. it & the sun.
orange & blue.
his father's hand conjoin-
ing
with an ear
left spare.

(iii) the living planet

seeder/combine. re-building
rain-washed spreads. the water deleterious & demi.
And all they've got to say
Is what a wonderful vista!
Not city lights absorbing
The stars – even the moon
Looks (more) vivid. Taut.　　here
Check out sun in summer's

　　　　　　　　　　centre

Comes the reply. I'll bet ya!
Cannot [any] lies well in randomness?

(iv) Expansion

lock stock and barrel
ie carrying its orbit in-
consistently.　　Note: key words. access?
Proper
bucketing
they gave him.
Proper. and they've electrified the railway
as well.
what the hell, he drank his first wine
at communion. transfixed: Kid's re-
call.

23 Na(rra)tive / *chapelle ardente*

Syz-23-key: uh oh
fetish or frou-frou
aza labels & ers on
artifize the case:
richter's rats struggle
& quickly
give up: identify. musical casing
setted. Up up up!

Rhe
-toric plans an
invest atations & calendars: grey
gunboats sweeping
dank rainforest rivers. patrons
of calypse & stoker
the moon drums UP tides: awash
melt-in-the-mouth } riprap.
& drawn out. ra ra ra.

isotopies
Id di
poussières
gestes
temps perdu tristan tzara
morphemic and trendy
up-
wards & categorise?

linger
mechaniser
'senex iratus'
swiftly
sits: progression towards
a system. Yes.

Yes.

logos
go go
& presuppose a % of
an *
[vraisemblance]
eschews a?

Touchy on a point
of picture & linkage = so what?
newstart with a kick
& get comfortable.

This case has potential: look,
they've got the drop
on you. De-
tailing
edifice &
scripture/s &
inspire-
ation: the sun brightens
    the shell grouting
    paving the lap lap
    of motoring stretched
    waves & sandbar circumflexed
    the pillars softly set
    and sinking, coming unstuck
    on soft-served banks, upwards
    & downwind the puckered hills
    glow like the haze. A fly
    settles on a fish corpse
and dies.

23.5 Pantoum

souwester blows cold
ha ha says granma
you'll chill to the bone
out there on the water

ha ha says granma
we gotta anyway
out there on the water
that's where goes sun & moon

we gotta anyway
cold when it oughta be hot
that's where goes sun & moon
burst & mix with blue

cold when it oughta be hot
we saw it in the telescope
burst and mix with blue
burnt dark like the road

we saw it in the telescope
granpa let us look
burnt dark like the road
and too close to lie

23 Lift

Ex hale and don't re-
(in) flate
                    it's dark
when you go out
{ing}   the fires
retract wetlands
breathe iced lakes
spoonbill & ibis
lurch-dance (in) space
{ing}   monograms
   [memory] re-
call the day, the weight
of light-lift, roll-back
sun buoyant
sienna-&-orange   luff & clouds & hills
obsessive and
manic * prone to out-
bursts
de rigueur
Ah! not love neat on the bus
I see {thru} your window/face
                    take
me back.

24 On

Oh ON!   loosely
never held   pivot(al) sans
      desire
on degeneration c/- object in
NO! touch me. On.

25 Urban Cross-over

Your soy coloured teeth
moth dust skin dys
function
-al: redress:
just a question
of supply: all roads lead in,
supply: all your
working daze: shopping trolleys
con-joining
in car-
parks.   Howzat?

26 Rural Patronising

Trill & twee wagtail lift
little nervous
nell-ies
take a break
at the heart the header
moves out over good soil
rippling like radiation
an electric
storm
spiriting
up-lifts,
& the fear
of fire & need for rain.

27 Intermission

I chase a hair
over my lip
trace it
with
tongue
& shiver spine deep and
hear my insides
recoil: a glass
to the wall!

28 Reality

If it's real it's been photo-
graphed but not by lips
testing on recall cauterised
word(s) – slash & burn, scorched
earth realising opacity
of skin and smooth cool sight
in our hands, wounds
washed & THE LAND
never sulking.

29 Link

Speech I link. Pro-
crastinate. 'Weialala leia'. Eh?
What did you say?
Can't make
head nor tail.
Of it: lyric?

30: re (con) structure ing / damage
control

(a)   Ponge c/- or à la Fahnestock

        ah
        'In this undergrowth, half shade half-sun
        Who thrusts these sticks between our spokes?'

>   river white burnt & scullcraft
>   taunting drift downtide, down
>   in the mouth & down towards
>   the centrifugal drag, & towed
>   & motored the sherry stained
>   ramps, I cry & laugh and palpitate

      & can

not right & moralise
& catastrophise & lies
out & about before sequestering
downs the spout & closes
the ment (al) gap: lash
out

                             no longer & yet
locate a shell of me like paving stones
zippy brass em[boss]-ing names
but not mine
god
willingly
the swells of pleasure lurid
& not a little jealous
of another era

                          seventy miles from here
                          where on lordly manors

clean hope
for forgiveness
but no more
blood below hook & rafter
becoming dirt

but
no more
cast in plaster
moulded joan   of arc   or jocaster
in revolutionary colours
caged & carved
                    biblical
red velvet fierce companions
perfect
eyes are missing
cont-
                    rol is
or has   been
dam(ag)ed:

quartz or nacre
lose lustre (less)
minutiae
packed & labelled
analytic & rolling
    fencewire
plugging gulleys

certain
even

        lichen covered rags
scrunched & welded
ARE dead parrots
sauve-qui-peut
    (!)

The point of impact
fabricates & inde
pend {ates}   enances – a disc plough
or slave cylinder
mixing mediums
with disaster
intra-personally: saltwash,
the creeks are storming
the river
& the crops are
waterlogged – melaleuca & salt scars
collaborate in a bundesfest
discordant
visits politely
call   ING   music
out-back. the tractor   ['wends its weary way]
no longer bushbashing
but suppurating spray
from soil, frisking
clean air
& tourists
warm in town   (as
                                Uncle Gerry
                                talks to Les Murray
                                who compares
                                Bunyah with

pasture
& a trio
of harmonists
make a go of friendship
without a tenor
providing a damn good
afternoon tea. You won't hear
cheques bouncing here. rather
sinking sand
& cockatoos.

& yes, we can hear the shutters
a-clicking & the chortle
of buses cruising down
the town's main street.

a stickler in a yella rain-jacket checkin'
the water troughs out in the rain
always wishing more sheep shelter
& the precise quantity & placement
of precipitate, as the tractor
sidles up to the silver fuel tank
& drinks.
this, I know. & re-
lease. the tractor is a star!
out here.

hot lead is introduced
to Crater Valley. Not True valley,
more of a deep deep creek between granite
and sandstone sweeps & high language shot & sheeted. crumble
lipping down to the York Gummed floor
& sheets split as sharp
as plough discs. of course.
For Crater Valley is also
The Valley of Foxes.
& they come, cousins & weekend hunters
& deplete.
& the need for locusts
as the third bell is raised
in its tower & God spits yellow
is begrudgingly ac-

                                        cepted.

& earth-tear
(as) families quake
stationwagons, earth snake
deep down & ripping up

Alien

hatchling.   old barn down
and (the) wells drained:
fresh gullies
ground thunder

groundwater thunders (complete)

despair
backstroking cross-lane or cutting the windrows
of THE childhood nightmare   I look
to the STREET
for a % -age & Age
& free (of)
tracasseries/   replete

(b) & Ponge / Fahnestock:

      'As also for
grass to straw,
or to the calamus for writing

to the pipe of "inspiration"
(…and to the straw in the "cocktail",
in the tall glass of the "long drink")'

the '&' is OUR angel.

Eh, balance up
spreadsheet
& paint on the carpet,
selling out
& making my almost (self)
<clear>. Eh, SPEAK UP
with subtlety:
I'm here & your practising virtue.

Eh, SPEAK UP
I can't hear & listen too quickly:

```
he shook the box
and could NOT
guess the contents.
```

Tractor parts.
Splinters from
THAT wagon wheel.
& a copy
of

POETRY

March 1966

Mary Ellen Solt: 'Flowers In Concrete'
'Magnificent
Aureoles
Rousing
Insensate
Grief
Oh
Long
Death
Suddenly'   #   here bottlebrush trees
drag blood out of cemeteries.

III

THE SILO

Rock Picking: Building Cairns

The spine is best kept straight –
the weight of granite will damage
vertebrae, stretch the spinal cord.
    Let the knees do the work,
legs levering the load from ground
to trailer dragged at a crawl behind
    the Massey Ferguson tractor.

Cairnwards we move over the paddock,
building these self-contained environments
for snakes, spiders, and bush-wise architects.
    Ground lost is ground gained,
these cairns are completely functional.
Satellite cities linked by machinery that's
    commuter friendly if unpredictable.

Rune stones carefully placed, oblatory,
offerings for local deaths – accidents at harvest,
on gravel roads, wild tractor's overturning,
augers catching a hand and swallowing flesh.
    And deities only farmers know.

Dried lichen and sweat mix to cement a cairn.
The surface suppressing the glitter of quartz –
pink, rose, white, transparent. Sources of warmth
these repositories of micro-chip technology
(unharnessed) attract infra-red telescopics,
blood coursing through their Frankenstein

monster bodies, distracting the predator's weapon
as it roams in search of foxes and rabbits.
Cairns – where youths empty swollen bladders
drunkenly into the fissures and cast amber bottles
into cobwebbed abysses, where wild oats grow at
impossible angles and lure the sun into darkness.

As I rock pick I unravel these pictures and spread
them to all corners of the paddock. I coin phrases,
devise anecdotes, invest the ups and downs of my
life in these cairns constructed from the landscape's
         wreckage, place sheep skulls on summits.

Alone, I feed these rowdy cities the stuff
of my blisters, sign the structures with broken
fingers, convert plans to ash and scatter
         them about the foundations.
Softly softly I sing the ruins of our
pampered anatomies, draw strength from the
         harsh realities of empire building.

And following duskfall, the tractor
and trailer no longer visible, I climb
onto the motorbike and drape myself over
         the seat – a bag of bones
slung over the tray of an iron jinker.
As the tractor comes into focus the cairns
         retreat – pyramids of the outback.

Collecting Wood near Williams Cemetery

Somebody's been here before
with a chainsaw. I collect raw
offcuts while my brother works larger blocks
with an axe so sharp it severs rocks,
he guards it like he does his shearing
gear – to hear it sing
as it splits the hardest wood
that its guarded force should
bring a soft and pleasant warmth.
The bitten wood breathes a resinous breath,
a raucous crow flies low
and we both look where it flew.
A short way down this gravel road
the local cemetery and a load
of stories. Pussy Reid, loved by
an entire town, knew he'd die
on a bike, was buried there
last year. We load the last block of melaleuca
and close the lid of the boot
on our work. I drive the silent
stretch to the cemetery
where Rottweilers are parked like Harleys
when Puss's mates come down to pay
respects. A mound conveys
a sense of flesh but flowers
and memories tower
above the barrow of gravel.
A honeyeater frisks amongst a spray of myrtle.
Eroded by heavy rains I suggest
that his soul will enrich the best
places water goes and Stephen
smiles brilliantly. A light rain
mists the light and growing cold
we turn to make for town,
there is a meal to be cooked
and wood to burn.

Brothers Trapping Parrots at Mullewa

Using an old bed base
propped in one corner
with a star picket
and sprung with a length
of cable from behind
the superphosphate shed,
two brothers
with the blessing
of their father
trapped flocks
of pink and grey galahs,
red and black tailed
cockatoos and Port
Lincoln parrots,
to take back
to city aviaries.
That these birds ripped
the flesh of their fingers,
themselves suffered pernicious
injuries, and eventually
perished in damp hessian sacks
slung in a boot and carried
four hundred miles,
didn't cross the brothers' minds
as the flocks winged into view,
moved with a unitary stealth
towards the plump yellow grain
spread over ground compressed
by dual-wheeled tractors
and semitrailers
with wheels taller
than children
older than themselves,
as they whipped the star picket
from its leverage,
sealed their consciences
with adrenalin.
Those dank sacks,
those birds looking

like tea-tree rubbed back
by cattle and sheep.
The look on their mother's
face, a storm mixed
and primed in Mullewa,
brought to Perth
in the boot of a car.

The Fire in the Forty-four

We're broke this week so my brother
collects aluminium cans and the copper
insides of old hot-water systems –
you need sacks of aluminium
cans to make even a few bucks
but a few kilos of copper or brass knocks
the price right up. It's dusk
as we approach the metalman behind his sooty mask,
storm clouds tinged crimson
and sitting low over his sheet-iron
shed, an almost virulent fire
sparking up in the pit of a forty-four
gallon drum. His sons pour
acetylene into the wounded guts
of a truck, like lightning putting to rights
damage done in some long past storm.
Outside a load of scrap looks almost warm
as it awaits the furnaces of the city.
Our metal is hooked in sacks to scales painfully
close to the fury of the drum.
To the pain of heat the metalman seems numb.
Though as he swings the singed sacks aside
before they burst into flame I note him hide
a softness behind his gauntlets of calluses,
the delicate timing, the dexterity as he tallies
payment rapidly on bone-black fingers.
A flurry of rain hisses deep in the drum
and spits back at the storm.
The metalman speaks in tongues to his vulcan
sons, who, deep in their alchemy, acknowledge only
with jets of flame. Quickly
he pays out and I follow my brother as he turns
away from the shed's darkening outline.

Harvest

1 Prayers and Charms

Harry spits blood at his crops on the eve of harvest –
warding off rain, high winds, excessive heat.
Jack takes a look over his shoulder and shoots
a cockatoo, divining weather's
intensity from the cast of its feathers,
Sue and Mary, their neighbours, interpret the stars
and are no longer the butts of jokes
in the district, they've been too accurate over the last
few seasons – even the Anglican minister
who puts a few acres in each year cocks an ear
when the gossip brings their predictions
floating through town.
Jack, it should be mentioned, also carries an amulet –
a good luck charm that's really a brass ring
that's losing its colour, as if the brass has been painted
over rusty iron and has begun to peel.
And of course a good few say their prayers
or cross their fingers or practise
strange rituals they've told no one about.

2 Dry Weather

And the headers are rolling through the crops
like electric shavers, the cut clean as the stalks
are dragged into the comb and the heads ripped
away, quail and snakes dispersing, the sun
sealing the cuts with a coppery swathe, the drivers
adjusting their headphones as dust drills the windows.
Children who have just finished exams check moisture
levels and signal that it's okay to continue.

3 Harvest Bans

Fire danger extreme.
The harvest bans
have been broadcast
and spread by word
of mouth. The bins
are closed until
late in the day
but still the
'don't-give-a-damn'
brigade push their
machines – flints
kindling the tinder.

Last season
one of them
was caught out
when a comb
hit an outcrop
of quartz
and sparked,
ten thousand acres
of crop going up
before volunteer
firefighters,
neighbours,
and some from
fifty miles away,
could extinguish
the sulky, persistent
flames. Even the field bins,
chock-a-block with the day's
ill-gotten gains, exploded
like grenades lobbed
from high ground.

4 Bins

Come the thunder of trucks
grain will whisper
through the grids.

Come the thunder of trains
we'll start the conveyors
and drain the bins.

We'll spear and sample –
count foreign bodies
under the keen eyes
of farmers,
check for ergot
as their features
grow ridiculously large.

Come the thunder of trains
we'll spread the tarps
and couple the wagons.

Come the thunder of trucks
we'll watch field mice
flicker amongst the stacks.

5 The Sunshine Harvester

There's a story behind that sunshine harvester
lodged amongst the twisted hands
of ruined harrows and the decayed teeth
of dingo traps. The owner's brother
had been pouring sacks of ungraded wheat
through its crazy teeth when the grain
like incense lulled his brain
and he fell deeply into the hopper,
into the header's violent breath.

6 Verandah and Watermelon

This year's wheat cheque
and a remarkable yield
on sand plain country
accompany slices
of watermelon
on the back verandah.
A daughter calculates
debt per equity ratio,
her brother listens
to the cricket score
on the radio.
A parrot drops
a set of nectarines
with its bolt-cutter beak
and the farmer doesn't
even move. His wife
looks nervously at
the rifle and waits.
More nectarines
and he doesn't seem
to care. What about
those markets? What's
happening with subsidies?
Went sixteen bags an acre
of sand plain country.
Well I'll be damned.

The Silo

Visitors, as if they knew, never remarked
on the old silo with its rammed earth walls
and high thatched roof, incongruous amongst
the new machinery and silver field bins.
Nor the workers brought in at harvest time,
trucks rolling past the ghostly whimperings,
snarls and sharp howls cutting the thick silo's
baffling. Nor when a bumper harvest filled
every bin and the farmer was hungry
for space – no one ever mentioned bringing
the old silo back into service. This
had been the way for as far back as could
be remembered. Thin sprays of baby's breath
grew around its foundations, while wedding
bouquet sprouted bizarrely from the grey
mat of thatching. The sun had bleached the walls
bone-white while the path to the heavily
bolted door was of red earth, a long thin
stream of unhealthy blood. Before those storms
which brew thickly on summer evenings
red-tailed black cockatoos settled in waves,
sparking the straw like a volcano, dark
fire erupting from the heart of the white
silo, trembling with energy deeper
than any anchorage earth could offer.
And lightning dragging a moon's bleak halo
to dampen the eruption, with thunder
echoing out over the bare paddocks
towards the farmhouse where an old farmer
consoled his bitter wife on the fly-proof
verandah, cursing the cockatoos, hands
describing a prison from which neither
could hope for parole, petition, release.

Parrot Deaths: Rites of Passage

Blue clouds scuttle the eucalypt sun
as it fizzes and winces with impending
rain, sultry weather dampening
the orange hearts of king parrots.

The scimitar roads cull the golden grain
from dump trucks and belly spillers, tarps
tethered loosely, illegal loads shifting
over axles tense with excess tonnage.

Rosellas gather about the grain offerings
and the torn bodies of the fallen. Wood smoke
hustles a magpie lark out of an uncharacteristic
torpor. A crow hangs low and watches intently.

Observing the rites of passage a regent
parrot plunges into the dead eyes of a semi,
eyes of silver nitrate, tarnished and stained
shadow black. The orange, golden and emerald

hearts of parrots litter the roads. I drive
slowly and whisper prayers of deflection.

The Fire in the Tail of the Cyclone

The tail of a cyclone stirs
and you fight back – shovel, hands, and wet
hessian. I see your funeral in the eyes
of sheep maddened with a lull in the wind:
rushing barbed wire fences, steamrolling
gates. Indoors, I taste it – the smell
forming an acrid film over my throat,
tongue, and lips. Like that mysterious
photograph I was telling you about
before the phonecall sparked in the
half-light and black smoke churned
through a turgid sky – 'Triumphal Entry
of the Bavarian Army into Munich', circa
eighteen seventy-one, where the army
is diminished and striped awnings
flap mockingly and the taste of victory
is the same taste I now experience.
Death is as is. The fire in the tail
of the cyclone cannot be read as writ,
and premonition is simply guilt.

IV

RECENT POEMS

Dissertation on a Wasp's Nest

Who that has Reason, and his Smell,
Wou'd not among Roses and Jasmin dwell?

– Cowley

1

Striking deep into the crisp
salvers of dead jasmine flowers
the paper wasp outpaces
the eye –
the elapsed witherings
of its avionics,
high pitched and devastating.

2

The nest of a paper wasp – thin grey
parchment chambers
moving towards opacity
bloom from a common
point, anchored stiffly
against the scent
of jasmine.

3

The wasp is the part
of a nest that flies.
Its wings the harp
on which frenzied
lullabies are cut.

4

A tiger with yellow stripes
would prefer to remain still
amongst the foliage,

85

watch as you pass confidently
by.
    As evening settles
like a fusty blanket, summer
heat pricking even the space
between carapace and skin,
the wasps move slowly
over the nest's chambers.
Even the full moon
lifting its yellow eye
over the rim of the fence
can revitalize them.
The pull of the sun
cannot be mimicked.

5

To separate a wasp's nest
from the jasmine – fierce
undertaking I should refuse,
but wishing to preserve
both it and my child's
inquisitive
and vulnerable flesh,
I seek merely
to transfer
to a place
safer for both.
Two wasps
and a nest
in a coffee jar:
an impression
in the moon's
limp light.

6

Moisture
from night waterings
lifts the lawns

and gardens
in the early morning.
Wasps' fire
in the coffee jar,
their nest precarious
on its glass floor,
holdfast swimming
the petrified current.

The Tiger Moth Poem

Prologue

High or low in the up & coming
Loop, the lift   lift   lift
Undercut & free of gravity:

Stress & tempestuous the cloud –
Material around the cowl & prop,
& the isolation as all eyes

Are fixed on you. And the sun
Low over your shoulder goading
You on & on and on, the blood

Too hot as a chill southern
Wind cuts past & you fly
By instinct, the instruments

All too crazy & the radio OUT.

1 Distance

Distant the lowland cutaway,
those mowed lines in the burnback;
red clay compatible under

the painfully blue
Autumn sky. It is seeding time
as I prepare to leave,

turn the climates upside down.
I leave the gneiss
& shale & lower

sheep jaws encased in fast
setting mud, cat prints
hot-trotting the pyrographed

lines of finches burnt
into the moistening straw,
the burrows of seed gatherers

foxes calling like crazy toys
that have lost their heads, pilots
learning *their* "tricks

of significance" in storming
the farmhouse roof, a windmill
centering the paddock.

I search for you. The compass's
tetchy needle disorientates
& the wind fates altitude.

I ground myself.

2 Those fractured & tempestuous flakes of sunlight

Darkness cannot seal the sky.
Highroller & naysayer
as night approaches

or bad weather sails
in from the coast. Joy
says stick it, hang in there.

I believe it. And can wait.

3 An Aside

Mount Bakewell prompts a flight
of cockatoos, furrows closely
cropped & sulphur crests

stirring flight as fear.
Ah, like snow ghosts
as blue as shadows

draped through leaves
they darken the road
with the intensity

of their navigations,
their individual brilliance
surrendered to instinct,

pandemonium, Babelic silos
coming unstuck, split grain
lighting the flock's heart.

4 Sculpturing hearsay

Once highrolling & sharp
& keeping it together
banks of wire
compile
a sculptural
ruse
as weekend pilots
pursue harmony
close to the ground
only to be dragged down
as the wire catches
their landing gear.

5 Zoom

Close-up you are as I
thought you might be;

focussed in your
secrecy.

6 South

Karri loam night-breathes.

Stars lift only to net
the canopy montage

while deeply emerald birds
rise vertically

dragging night backwards.

7 A definition of space

Positioning ourselves
between lovers,
delaying flights,
letting sleep shape
a life between the covers.

8 Skippy Rock

Ground to antimony
cuttlefish long-since
scuttled on Skippy Rock,
oyster catchers & sulky
fishhooks lodged between rock
& froth. A phalanx
of red rock crabs
backtracking as the swell
tests their grip & we
invoke freak waves
expecting them to tell
us something about our-
selves. A Tiger Moth
flies against the sun
& touches your
outstretched finger,
the whirr of its engine
an affirmation as love
inclines naturally

towards the möbius thread
binding rock & sea & air
& the brilliant red beaks
of the oyster catchers
pierce the pretty
picture.

9 (i) Ascension

Smoke sitting at thirty degrees
to an indigo sea
drives you inland
where swans familiar
with the chatter
of de-Havilland
refuse to rise
from placid waters
that hold Molloy Island
firmly in their grip.
The best time is before the sun
drinks stars that have drunk the sea,
when cowboys are crashed out
& the larvae of tiger moths
sense wings stretching
over their bodies – the brilliance
of their markings suggesting
a delicate winter but one bitter
for predators. Time
cannot exceed 139 knots
per hour & the journey
must be worth its destination
as rivets & split pins spin wildly
in stall, climb, or cruise,
& the world of trawlers, nets, and jetties
is micro, & a brickred sunset is a wall
dissolving with an arrival
timed by flights
of pelicans.

9 (ii) Even the sewage ponds look beautiful

Even the sewage ponds
look beautiful from up here –
over the perfectly framed
& textured glassine
surface, discolouration
the mystery in a brilliantly vivid
Guy Grey-Smith
                    painting.

10 "It was a store of the unspoken in the bird
    that whirred the air, that every
            occasion of the word
        overawed."

Robert Duncan

It is said over Sugarloaf Rock near the Cape
that a red-tailed tropic bird fails
            to land & passes
its southern-

most breeding ground. That it flies against its instinct
to re-join its programmed flight, to
            stir warming thermals
against the cold

words that define its plight. That you remain silent
as I recount the facts, the light
            stripped back & season-less,
night-bound &

choked up.

11 Anomalies

Clouds deeply navy
disorientate & pin
tiger moths to spires.

Zinc clouds strung high lift
wing-torn tigermoths gently
from spires, just because.

Sun dials heli-pads
back flying to avoid spires
in life-saving flight.

12 A Prayer of Thanks

to sing with spirit & mind
that flesh is yours & penitent
& escaping the autolystic,
auto-da-fé,
the fuel that brought fire
without warmth,
the flight bound-down
by topography,
that you taught me to honour the body.

Self-Portrait without Glasses

1

I am outside
& the rain
has blown the rusty
guttering
doused the fig tree,
porch light ghosting
squat concrete
columns
that would make
this porch different –
architects specializing
in duplexes are conscious
of things like this,
even in low-income
areas – familiar
as I am
with these
surroundings
I remove my glasses
& re-interpret – the squat
becomes a lazy streak
condensing
minus
five dioptre – a squint
that will not focalize
Corinthian
or lay at length
the Waldeck Nursery
monotony

2

A chilli merges
with the glowing tip
of a skywriting
cigarette – trans

firefly or lip slippage
premeditating
a meteorite fizzing
down thru the outer
atmosphere.

Landscapes
merge
& concepts
associate
with blocks
of colour.

Floodlit in an open window
& "you'll catch
your death": the sound
isn't heightened
but there are variables
of light.

3

Roadkill & G-locking:
I stagger amongst cars
streaming the highway's
Möbius strip:
crime qua crime
but not in full possession
of the facts
I feel compelled to drop
the case: good sight
IS intransigent,
despite the forecaster's
radar-echoes
scripted as paling & palsy
cops too pissed
to give evidence
after a record
bust.

4

I sense too a neighbour
wondering about rain & shadow
only Frankenthaler could
with confidence instil
rooms as inking puddles
& without my glasses
I might shuffle forward
& fall – like my son
who says that television
shows lolly-bloated children
sinking though the floor.

A (C)ode for Simon Templar

"He's having so much fun
        speaking code
But he can't tell you
        what it's for – "
                The Celibate Rifles, *Les Fusils Celibataires*

"The weather is syntax
Thus we can speak of a cold of poetry"
                Lyn Hejinian, *Oxota*

A strange cold blew out
of distress, and sleep ignored you: good thing

it was then and only then (I)
turned up: my long neglected

country house full of obje(c)t d'
art and tasteless – comes of absence

and my housekeeper calling (sic).
Gets right to the bones, this diamond

frost like razor wire, a trap sprung
from inside like all good/proper

sex, which is me-mory; shall we?
They might call this the Russian way:

negating and coming down though
I like your kid gloves anyway –

or am I just moving my lips,
you Americans like it both

ways plus, as for myself a bouquet
of roses, no maybe (only) three:

yellow for friendship, pink for love,
and red for lust, no, make that passion.

Hey, this just doesn't sound familiar,
unless hanging out at Bondi

has rendered me
useless in the eyes of polite

society, but Christ, did I
lord it over those Aussies:

my alabaster skin, halo
of antimony, snappy

dress sense, ability to make
clever jokes about Marx, Mao and Ché.

Erratum

Every link (is) a separation.

> "and this the
> floodloam, the deposit, borrowed for
> the removal. Call it inland, his
> nose filled with steam & his brief cries."
>   J H Prynne, *Aristeas, in Seven Years*

panchromatics: testy sundial
intersecting a bright array
less necessary (non-plussed) than
sight or loss as pages
help selves confer centre-
pieces like a jigged inward
road they've long since [lost]

fineprint in silent over-
tones, trast gnomic & heuristic godpath
loves still as all is well
& goodly politics dwell as audit
(tory) truth allusively: sand-$s
& expeditions as dead in deader trees

the river's swerve as oft is shored
against the surfaced strain,
in cleft & vein, text urs a looping
range, we cross the bridge in iron sur-
rounds, opaline a compass'
s doom, popular & pyritic the dry bed turns

?: light gives what, directs as form,
sinecure or set the leafy frame: time not been
in lisping ana-strains: red dust stuffs the pans
& boats are nothing short of crazed:
stuck as the bloody compass!

tributary empire gutted as imperial
craft bad taste the furthest flung & busy
cases: ration (that diatribe) hook across
the watershed & laugh the ebb
of ancient language: I innate Le langage, cet
inconnu, & respect no prop
or stolen nouns: the charts re(ad) up-
side down

links as loose as solvent[s-at] parties
Azev-vous une pièce d'identité: violent/
corri(gend)um via the surgical scan-
ning, subterfuge & malicious group
ing of words, space left as calmatives:
rare species of birds drinking (only) sand

riparian la high water marks a Southron accent
against the loving policy: crush not the
equal body or holy-weighted equi
librium, all tenure & scud, the combing showers.

dunes do fume, the poet said, sidecut mainsails a-bolting
kedge, the graphs or frame hard spoken, oilskins
dredging the babbled pentecost as speech pre & post
binds the universal congregation:

inner, time to collect the hay as bales
pyro black in plastic (what should) be a brilliant day, the soil
as clean as water locked away
impedimenta & hush hush against the hol-
low rock, dieresis(tic) tic tic the foäm as red
as sheets of slough &
long-range drought

drag-hooked again
the quasi-structures,
skim the typos, cadenza,
river's slipshod
utterings

The Police Busted Me with a Chilli in my Pocket

It'd been through the wash – it was
in fact half-a-chilli
looking fibrous and not a little
washed out. But there was
no doubting it was a chilli,
I accepted that – no need
for laboratory tests, the eye
and honesty adequate analysis.
So, why do you do it
they asked. I *dunno*, just a habit
I guess. The sun dropped below
the horizon like a billiard ball.
The chilli glowed in a hand.
One of them rubbed his eyes and they
began to sting. We'll have you for assault
they said.

Warhol at Wheatlands

He's polite looking over the polaroids
saying gee & fantastic, though always
standing close to the warm glow

of the Wonderheat as the flames
lick the self-cleansing glass.
It's winter down here & the sudden

change has left him wanting. Fog
creeps up from the gullies & toupées
the thinly pastured soil. It doesn't

remind him of America at all. But there's
a show on television about New York so
we stare silently, maybe he's asleep

behind his dark glasses? Wish Tom
& Nicole were here. He likes the laser
prints of Venice cluttering the hallway,

the sun a luminous patch trying
to break through the dank cotton air
& the security film on the windows.

Deadlocks & hardened glass make him feel
comfortable, though being locked inside
with Winchester rifles has him tinfoiling

his bedroom – he asks one of us but we're
getting ready for seeding & can't spare a moment.
Ring-necked parrots sit in the fruit trees

& he asks if they're famous. But he
doesn't talk much (really). Asked about Marilyn
he shuffles uncomfortably – outside, in the

spaces between parrots & fruit trees
the stubble rots & the day fails
        to sparkle.

Black Suns

The orchard, canker-bound and fading – Australian
Gothic. A bladeless windmill remonstrates

with a warm wind as it singes
oranges scattered in bitter wreaths

of deadwood, scale, and vitrified leaves.
A black-winged kite wrestles with temptation

and logic – water rats scaling the ruins
of barbed wire fences. The season equivocates.

I remove my shoes, the water stretches
bulrushes like new strings on an old guitar.

I position the wreck of my body and wait.
There is arrogance in this – expecting

him to appear, to consider his withering fruit,
divine my return, while refusing to cross

and help drag black suns from their sick zodiacs
with the hook of his walking stick.

Wireless Hill

Not seen for decades the parrot bush
made a subtle comeback – fire
liberating seeds from their long

hibernation. A twenty eight melds
into its birth flower, camouflaging
and buzzing and cackling out of sight:

a satellite lost in crazy telemetry,
untrackable despite an atmosphere
of communication. The sea breeze, salty

and moist and full of static, zips
about the walkways and the triptych
of lookout towers, anchorage blocks

of Wireless Hill's original aerial.
With a festive glint on their bonnets,
cars unwind the radials, stereos

pursue their fractious circuits, trilling
and hissing like valve radios. And from
the central tower I look out over

Alfred Cove, and absorb the river.
You watch the children ski down slides
in the adventure playground and scoot

their bikes about the walkways, the sticky
hum that comes with rubber on hot concrete
reminding you of our son. You look

to the base of the tower, I look out –
even further than the river. But the sun
drives us towards the shade and touching

earth we hear the silent conversations
that crackle so faintly, too faint even
for aerials to detect. Yes, our son
106

would wade out into that cove,
over the rusty flats, bloodworms
unravelling and inciting black silt,

while pelicans, those navigation
markers for waders and migratory birds,
disappear in the space between sandbars.

Skippy Rock, Augusta: Warning, the Undertow

1

Oyster catchers
scout the tight rutilic
beach rust charting

run-off locked
cross-rock up-coast
from the bolted

lighthouse
where two oceans
surge & rip & meet.

2

Immense the deep lift
seizes in gnarls & sweeps,
straight up & built

of granite. A black
lizard rounds & snorts
the froth capillaried

up towards dry-land's
limestone, hill-side
bone marrow mapped

by water. Meta-wrought,
the lighthouse distantly
elevates & turns

the crazily
bobbing history
of freak waves

and wrecks: wrought-iron
& lead paint brewing
deep in capsized

sealanes, talking shop
in thick clots of language,
bubbles thundering topwards.

3

The stab-holes
of fishing poles,
small-boy whipping

boy those gate-
crashing waves releasing
shoals of wrecked

cuttlefish bleeding sepia
like swell prising
the weed-swabbed rocks

& darkly crescented beach:
crabclaw & limpet
scuttlebut

about the rubbery
swathes of kelp.
Tenebrous lash

& filigreed canopy
of dusk-spray, undertow
of night.

Tide Table

Oddly levelled diaspora
& flight I cannot be defined
it says, chromatic
as only a special camera
might capture
a tiger moth, amongst the linen
or imprisoned
in brilliant & solitary flight –
the tidal blood or necessary
flowing: that every diversion
wandering
sudden change in direction
caused by a predatorial threat
has and will be written. The sum total of
all tidal leanings in the blood,
the nervous system,
gyroscopic
is love.

Lowflying the flood
or woodsmoke
in the burnt offerings
of past lives
or propositions
or hoped-for destinations.
We have arrived nowhere
but hope to move on.
The flood
the highwater mark,
shed like the collective call cards
or whirr and delays
C/- satellites,
whom about, about whom,
we circulate
but never orbit – that's gravitational
and the effort to break free
will damage this delicate
wing
structure.